MW00488586

Landauer Books

This book was designed, produced,
and published by Landauer Books
A division of Landauer Corporation
3100 NW 101st Street, Urbandale, Iowa 50322
www.landauercorp.com 800/557-2144

President: Jeramy Lanigan Landauer
Director of Sales & Operations: Kitty Jacobson
Editor-in-Chief: Becky Johnston
Managing Editor: Jeri Simon
Art Director: Laurel Albright
Photographer: Craig Anderson

Creative Director: Lynette Jensen
Art Director: Kate Grussing
Photostyling: Lynette Jensen
Technical Writer: Sue Bahr
Technical Illustrator: Lisa Kirchoff

We also wish to thank the support staff of the Thimbleberries® Design Studio:
Sherry Husske, Virginia Brodd, Renae Ashwill, Ardelle Paulson,
Julie Jergens, Clarine Howe, Tracy Schrantz, Amy Albrecht, and Leone Rusch.

The following manufacturers are licensed to sell Thimbleberries® products:
Thimbleberries® Rugs (www.colonialmills.com);
Thimbleberries® Quilt Stencils (www.quiltingcreations.com);
Thimbleberries® Sewing Thread (www.robison-anton.com); and
Thimbleberries® Fabrics (RJR Fabrics available at independent quilt shops).

Cover: Instructions for making the Garden Glory quilt are included
in the Thimbleberries® Quilting a Patchwork Garden book.

THIMBLEBERRIES®
My Quilts

Garden Glory

Keeping a journal about your quilts…

Of the hundreds of quilts I've designed down through
the years, the ones I recall most vividly are those that
were made to share with loved ones. Handmade quilts
given with love represent every quilter's hope and faith
in the future, and what better way to preserve that
heritage than with a journal filled with memories of your
favorite quilts.

Every quilt has a story to tell and holds special memories
for its maker. In the past, a handmade quilt was a special
gift, treasured for a lifetime, and carefully preserved
for the next generation. Today, you can carry on that
tradition with a photo journal designed for photographs
and recording memories of the special quilts you've
made—whether for yourself or for friends and family.

This journal is conveniently sized to accommodate a
standard 4x6-inch photograph with plastic zipper pockets
for storing swatches of the fabrics used to make your
quilts—all in a hidden loose-leaf, refillable binding with

pages printed on acid-free paper to protect the contents for the future. You'll want to use acid-free tape for securing your photographs and an acid-free pen for recording your memories to create a treasured keepsake.

Throughout the pages of this journal you'll find photographs offering a closer look at the details of a dozen delightful quilts I've designed for Thimbleberries®. Each of the quilts reflects a favorite theme or season that has inspired the quilts—from spring and summer to harvest and holidays.

For a starting point, begin by filling the pages of this journal with photographs of quilts that celebrate your own favorite memories. Then take a few moments to reflect and record your memories of those special occasion quilts. Keep in mind that whether your quilt is made to keep or give to others, the memories it holds will stay in hearts forever. Wishing you more wonderful quilting memories than your heart can hold…

My best,

Lynette Jensen

Instructions for making this quilt are included in the Thimbleberries® Quilting a Patchwork Garden book.

Sage
Garden
Patch

My Photo Here

My Quilt

My Photo Here

My Quilt

My Photo Here

My Quilt

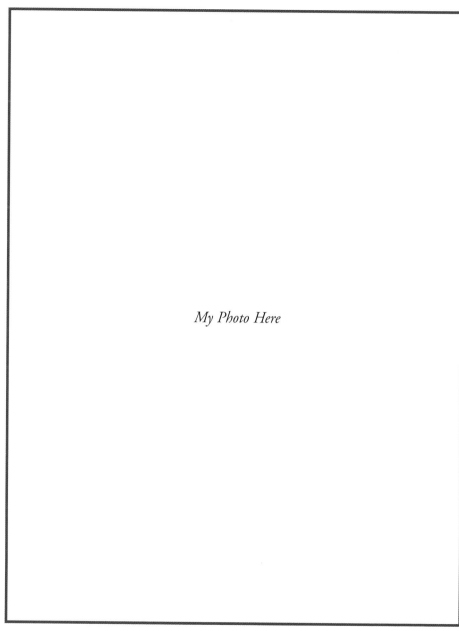

My Photo Here

My Quilt

Instructions for making this quilt are included in the Thimbleberries® Quilts for My Sister's House book.

Puzzle Perfect

My Photo Here

My Quilt

My Photo Here

My Quilt

My Photo Here

My Quilt

My Photo Here

My Quilt

Instructions for making this quilt are included in the Thimbleberries® Quilting a Patchwork Garden book.

My Photo Here

My Quilt

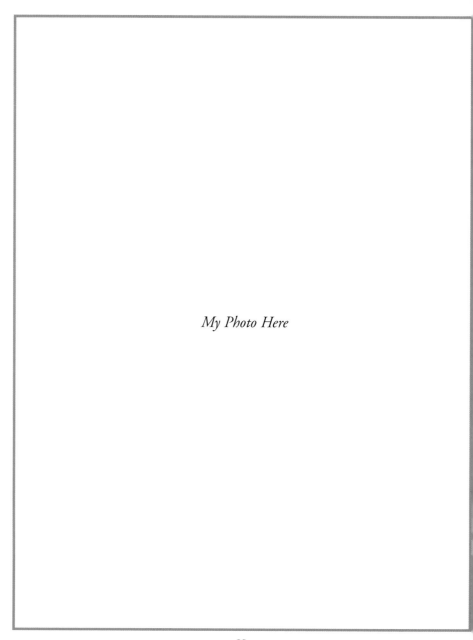

My Photo Here

My Quilt

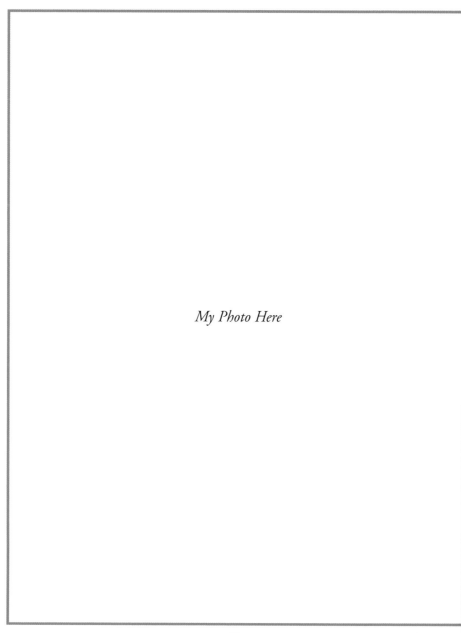

My Photo Here

My Quilt

My Photo Here

My Quilt

Instructions for making this quilt are included in the
Thimbleberries® Quilting a Patchwork Garden book.

Summertime

My Photo Here

My Quilt

My Photo Here

My Quilt

My Photo Here

My Quilt

My Photo Here

My Quilt

Instructions for making this quilt are included in the Thimbleberries® Quilting a Patchwork Garden book.

Tulip
Patch

My Photo Here

My Quilt

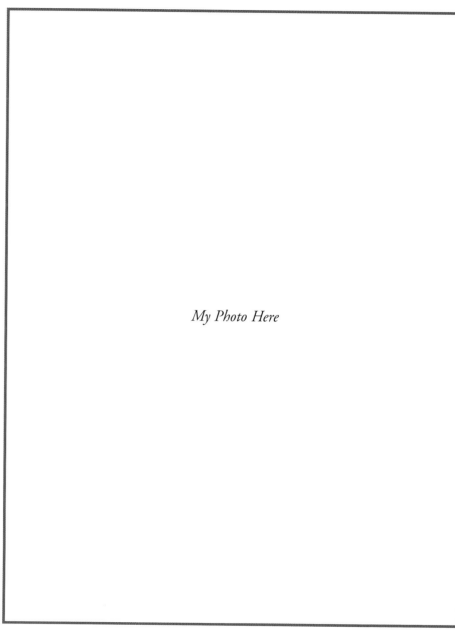

My Photo Here

My Quilt

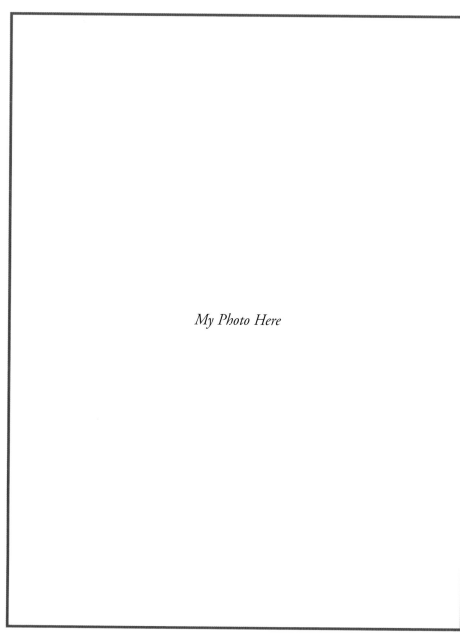

My Photo Here

My Quilt

My Photo Here

My Quilt

Instructions for making this quilt are included in the Thimbleberries® Quilting a Patchwork Garden book.

My Photo Here

My Quilt

My Photo Here

My Quilt

My Photo Here

My Quilt

My Photo Here

My Quilt

Instructions for making this quilt are included in the
Thimbleberries® Quilts for My Sister's House book.

Fancy
Flywheels

My Photo Here

My Quilt

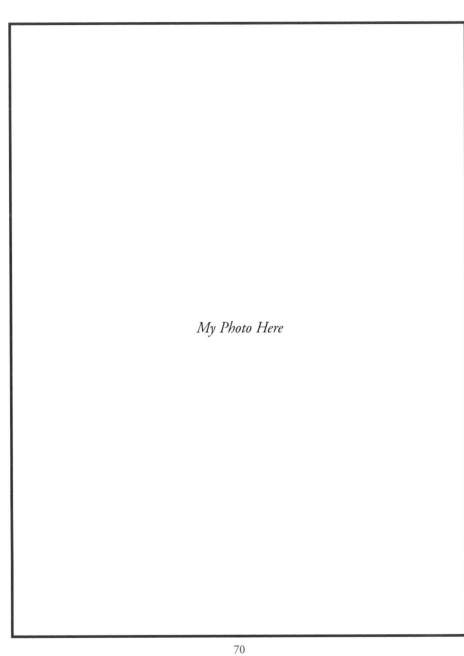

My Photo Here

My Quilt

My Photo Here

My Quilt

My Photo Here

My Quilt

Instructions for making this quilt are included in the
Thimbleberries® Quilting a Patchwork Garden book.

Autumn Runner

My Photo Here

My Quilt

My Photo Here

My Quilt

My Photo Here

My Quilt

My Photo Here

My Quilt

Instructions for making this quilt are included in the
Thimbleberries® Quilts for My Sister's House book.

Nature Walk

My Photo Here

My Quilt

My Photo Here

My Quilt

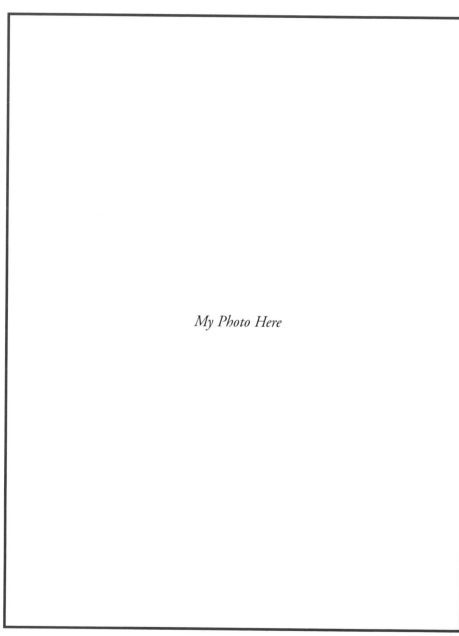

My Photo Here

My Quilt

My Photo Here

My Quilt

Instructions for making this quilt are included in the
Thimbleberries® Quilting a Patchwork Garden book.

Paddlewheel Surround

My Photo Here

My Quilt

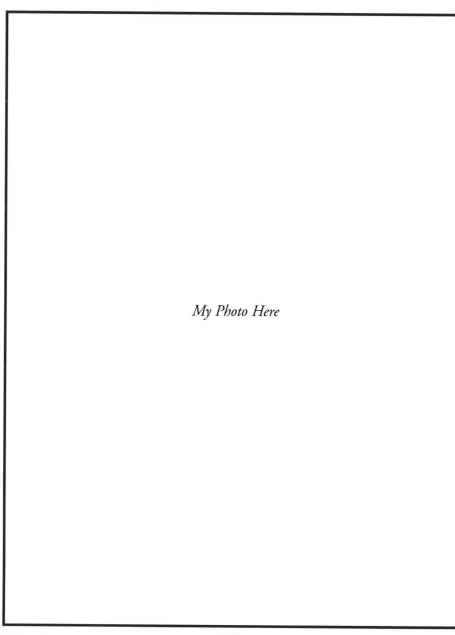

My Photo Here

My Quilt

My Photo Here

My Quilt

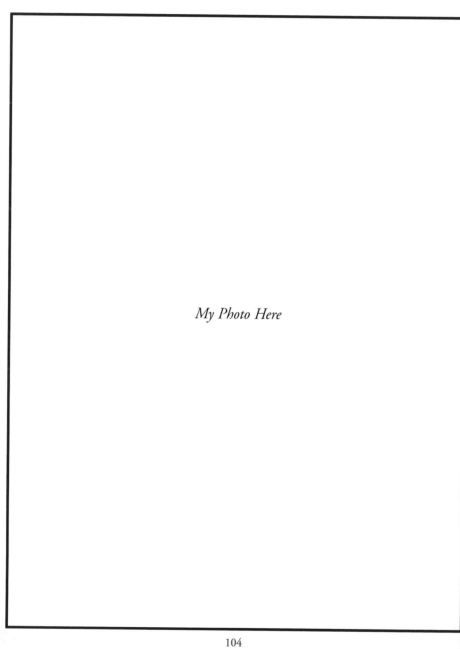

My Photo Here

My Quilt

Instructions for making this quilt are included in the Thimbleberries® Quilting a Patchwork Garden book.

Chevron Log Cabin

My Photo Here

My Quilt

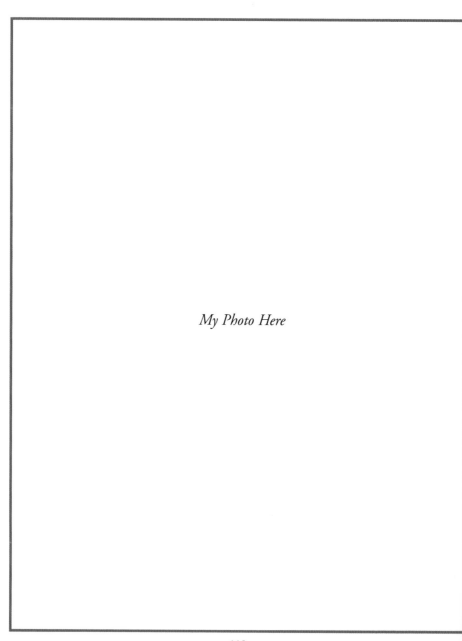

My Photo Here

My Quilt

My Photo Here

My Quilt

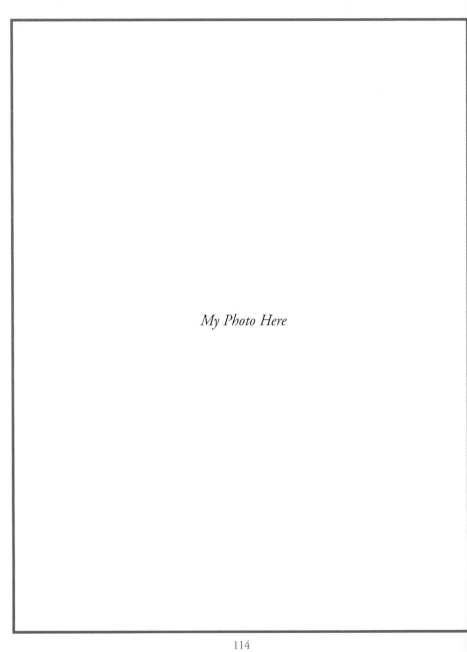

My Photo Here

My Quilt

Instructions for making this quilt are included in the
Thimbleberries® Quilts for My Sister's House book.

Cherry Berry

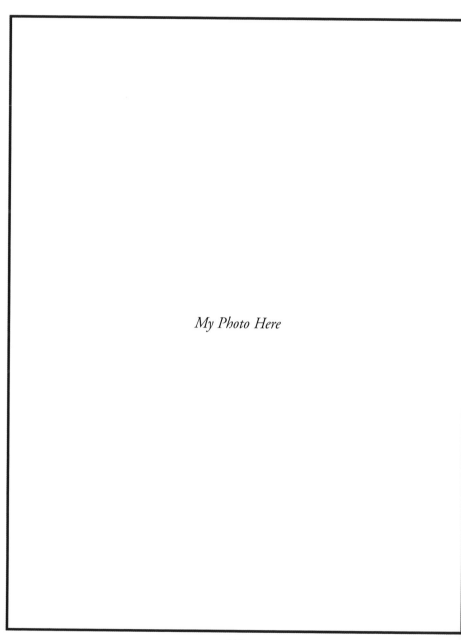

My Photo Here

My Quilt

My Photo Here

My Quilt

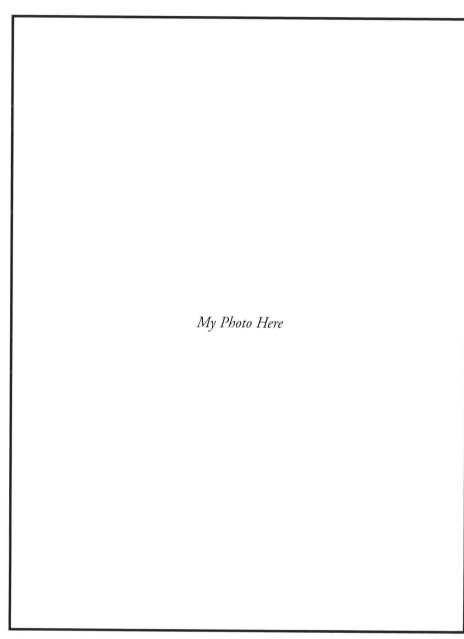

My Photo Here

My Quilt

My Photo Here

My Quilt

About
Lynette Jensen

Lynette Jensen is recognized as a leading fabric designer in the independent quilt industry, the best-selling author of dozens of books with nearly a million copies sold, and a foremost educator and authority on the subject of quilting and decorating and helping others create a home that "hugs you back."

Lynette has been at the forefront of the home arts as president of her highly visible company, Thimbleberries®, which offers consumers coordinating fabric print collections and the ability to put them together in a clear, graphic sense to create a hand-quilted product they can be proud of.

Another successful component in the Thimbleberries® brand mix is the Thimbleberries® Club which reaches tens of thousands of quilters. Many years ago Lynette launched the Club program that has been welcomed by nearly 1,000 independent shop owners who conduct in-store Clubs for thousands of quilters.

Designing from her traditional point of view, Lynette introduces six to eight collections a year in all-cotton and flannel. In addition to fabric and books, licensed products include rugs, embroidery cards, stencils and thread.

Whether designing, decorating, gardening, entertaining, cooking or crafting, Lynette, who lives with her husband Neil in a beautifully restored home in Hutchinson, Minnesota, does it well with warmth and humor.

Thimbleberries® Books by Lynette Jensen
Recent Releases

Thimbleberries® books are available at bookstores, fabric and craft stores.
If you are unable to find them at your favorite retailer, contact
Landauer Corporation at 1-800-557-2144 or visit www.landauercorp.com

**Thimbleberries® Quilting
a Patchwork Garden**
ISBN: 978-1-890621-62-9

**Thimbleberries® Quilts
for My Sister's House**
ISBN: 978-1-890621-57-5

**Thimbleberries® Learning
to Quilt with Jiffy Quilts**
ISBN: 978-1-890621-51-3

**Thimbleberries®
Photo-Ready Scrapbook**
ISBN: 978-1-890621-54-4

**Thimbleberries® New
Collection of Classic Quilts**
ISBN: 978-1-890621-98-8

**Thimbleberries®
Collection of Classic Quilts**
ISBN: 978-1-890621-88-9

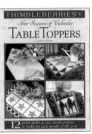

**Thimbleberries® Four Seasons
of Calendar Table Toppers**
ISBN: 978-0-9770166-8-6

**Thimbleberries®
Quilting for Harvest**
ISBN: 978-1-890621-16-2

**Thimbleberries® Big
Book of Quilt Blocks**
ISBN: 978-1932533-05-7

**Thimbleberries®
Beginner's Luck**
ISBN: 978-0972558-01-3

**Thimbleberries®
Pint-Size Traditions**
ISBN: 978-1932533-03-3

**Thimbleberries® Oh Sew
Cozy Flannel Quilts**
ISBN: 978-1932533-04-0